Photographing the Second Gold Rush

Photographing the Second Gold Rush

Dorothea Lange and the East Bay at War, 1941–1945

Introduction by Charles Wollenberg

Heyday Books, Berkeley, California

Publisher's Cataloguing in Publication
   (prepared by Quality Books, Inc.)
Photographing the second gold rush : Dorothea Lange and the East Bay
   at war 1941–1945 / introduced by Charles Wollenberg.
      p. cm.
      Includes bibliographical references.
      ISBN 0-930588-78-9

   1. San Francisco Bay Area (Calif.)--History. 2. World War,
1939–1945--San Francisco Bay Area (Calif.) 3. Lange, Dorothea. 4.
Documentary photography--History.   I. Lange, Dorothea.

F868.S156P46 1995   979.4'052
                                 QBI95-20399

Photograph of Dorothea Lange on page 6 courtesy of Library of Congress. All other photos courtesy of the Oakland Museum, Oakland, California.

Interior and cover design: Jeannine Gendar

Printed in the United States of America
10 9 8 7 6 5 4 3 2 1

Acknowledgments

Thanks to Drew Johnson and Therese Heyman for their cooperation in making available the photographs from the Oakland Museum collection. I also appreciated the assistance of Elizabeth Partridge and the willingness of Jerry Herman to read the manuscript. Finally, thanks to the hard-working staff of Heyday Books and to their boss, Malcolm Margolin, for his support, collaboration, conversation, and free (albeit cheap) lunches. —C. W.

This newspaper photograph was taken at a relocation center for people of Japanese descent in San Francisco, in 1942. Dorothea Lange is in the background, with camera. She "had a peculiar facility for just melting away and for not seeming to be photographing at the same time she was sticking a camera in somebody's face."

Introduction

Charles Wollenberg

"All ages, races, types, skills and backgrounds. A deluge of humanity." That was how Dorothea Lange described the scene of workers leaving the Kaiser Richmond shipyards during a shift change in 1944. It might well have been a description of the tide of social change that swept the Bay Area during World War II. In historian Marilynn Johnson's words, the war was a "Second Gold Rush," a watershed event that defined a whole era of Bay Area history much as the first Gold Rush had done a century earlier. In the war years, the Bay Area population grew by a half million people, an increase of 35 percent in just five years. Since many of the newcomers were African Americans and Latinos, the Bay Area grew in ethnic diversity even more dramatically than in population. These demographic changes drastically affected the everyday lives of Bay Area communities. Richmond, for example, "took a beating," according to *Fortune* magazine. The streets were crowded with "gaping strangers in cowboy hats, blue jeans, and sombreros." One longtime resident recalled: "I used to greet everyone on the street. Now I don't even look for a familiar face when I step out of my office."

Dorothea Lange, the region's finest documentary photographer, photographed this Second Gold Rush, working out of her home in the Berkeley Hills. While she took pictures throughout the Bay Area, most of her images are of East Bay locations, the majority in Oakland and Richmond. This book includes sixty of her wartime photographs, chosen from the hundreds that exist in her personal files now at the Oakland Museum. Some of the images have been previously published, but this is the first time they have been grouped together in a single volume. As such, they are an important historical document, a pictorial interpretation of the beginning of the defense era and the resulting social and demographic transformation of a major American metropolitan region.

"A very interesting job, a trade"

By the time World War II began, Dorothea Lange was already one of the nation's leading documentary photographers. Born in 1895, she was raised in Hoboken, New Jersey. She suffered a serious case of polio at age seven which left her right leg permanently crippled. Sixty years later, she commented, "I was physically disabled, and no one who hasn't lived the life of a semi-cripple knows how much that really means." When she was twelve, her father left the household, and she eventually adopted her mother's family name and used it the rest of her life. The most influential person in her early childhood was her maternal grandmother, whom Dorothea described as a "temperamental, difficult, talented woman," a description that might apply to Dorothea herself in later years. By contrast, she described her mother as "more dependent on me than I was on her." Her mother told her, "you have much more iron in you than I have." "And," said Dorothea, "it's true."

When she was in the seventh grade, her mother worked as a librarian in New York City's Lower East Side, and Dorothea commuted with her each day, attending a nearby public school in which she was the only gentile in an otherwise Jewish student body. In the library after school, she neglected her lessons, preferring to "read every book." Lange eventually transferred to an uptown private school, an institution she described as a "miserable high school." She often cut classes, wandering for hours around the city, observing and absorbing the vibrant street life. She contended that "it wasn't an unproductive truancy. I know that city. I know cities. And I'm not afraid to be alone."

By the time she graduated from high school in 1914, Dorothea was a strong-willed, intelligent young woman. Small and attractive, she had a pronounced limp, luminous eyes, and a narrow, expressive face. To her family's surprise, she announced that she wanted to be a photographer, even though she had never taken a picture and did not own a camera. The family insisted that she enroll in a teachers' college, but before long she had dropped out to devote herself full-time to her dream of a photographic career. Although she took a photography course from Clarence White at Columbia University, most of her knowledge of the craft was gained from hands-on experience in jobs at a number of commercial studios. "I learned the trade, you see, through many people. I guess I was sort of a sponge."

She explained that she never intended to become an "artist." "I've always thought of myself—and in these years also—as finding ways to learn what I thought was a very interesting job, a trade."

In 1917, at the age of 22, she and a friend embarked on what was supposed to be a round-the-world trip. She said, "It was a matter of really testing yourself out." The test wasn't entirely successful; six weeks later, the two young women found themselves flat broke in San Francisco. They took jobs, Dorothea as a clerk in a stationery and photo finishing store. Over the counter, she met photographer Imogen Cunningham and her husband, Roi Partridge, beginning more than four decades of friendship with multiple generations of the Partridge clan. Through the Partridges, Dorothea joined a camera club and was introduced into San Francisco's lively bohemia. In 1918 friends staked her to an independent portrait photography business and she opened a studio in downtown San Francisco.

Two years later, Dorothea married Maynard Dixon, a well-known San Francisco artist and member of the bohemian scene who was 21 years her senior. For the next decade and a half, she said that "the largest part of my energy, and my deepest allegiances, were to Maynard's work, and my children" [sons Daniel and John]. Yet, even in these years, Dorothea reserved for herself "a small portion of my life... and that was my photographic area." She continued to operate her studio, developing a distinguished clientele that included some of the city's wealthiest and most influential families. For the rest of her life, she agonized over the conflict between her role as wife and mother and the obligations of her photographic career. She believed that a "woman's position is immeasurably more complicated" than a man's. "I would like to have one year.... Just one when I would not have to take into account anything but my inner demands."

In the early 1930s, the economic burdens of the Depression and, perhaps, the personal burdens of a sometimes difficult marriage, persuaded Dixon and Lange to give up their house and move into their respective studios, about a block apart on Montgomery Street in San Francisco. This required putting their sons in a Marin County boarding school, something Lange found "very, very hard for me to do." In 1933 and 1934, she began photographing outside of the studio, shooting scenes of the intense social drama that was playing itself out on the streets of San Francisco. Her subjects included impoverished men in bread lines, political demonstrations, and the great labor battles that culminated in the 1934 General Strike. She was taking pictures that were later to make her famous and, in the process, helping to invent the modern genre of documentary photography. Soon the documentary work came to dominate her life: "I was taking portraits to finance this other work, and to take care of the boys."

"Paul is my rock"

Paul Taylor, an Economics Professor at the University of California, first saw Dorothea's work at an informal Oakland exhibition in 1934. Impressed by the visual images of social conditions and conflict, Taylor asked if he could use one of the photographs to illustrate an article he was writing. He later invited Lange and a few other Bay Area photographers, including Imogen Cunningham, to accompany him on a research trip to a cooperative lumber mill in the Sierra foothills. An activist Jeffersonian liberal who had little use for "ivory tower" scholarship, Taylor accepted a position with the state division of the Federal Emergency Relief Agency to do field studies of conditions of rural poverty. Believing that "*words* would not be enough to show the conditions vividly and accurately," he conspired to hire Dorothea to make photographs for his reports. Since there was no budget for a photographer, he initially put her on the payroll as a typist (even though she couldn't type).

Lange quickly proved her worth to the agency, and in 1934 and 1935 she made several trips with Taylor, sometimes with Maynard Dixon tagging along. Later in 1935, she obtained a full-time position with the federal Resettlement Agency. A New Deal institution devoted to ameliorating rural poverty and social dislocation, it became the Farm Security Agency in 1937. Under historical director Roy Stryker, the FSA gathered a crew of immensely talented photographers, including Dorothea, to document rural conditions and publicize the agency's work. Taylor was now doing field studies for the Social Security Board, and the two federal bureaucracies approved joint research expeditions so that Lange and he could continue a productive working collaboration that was also becoming an intense personal relationship. In December 1935, after obtaining uncontested divorces from their spouses, Lange and Taylor married in Albuquerque, New Mexico. Taylor reported that "on the afternoon of the same day," Dorothea "went out and photographed. And our work went on, together."

The marriage began an extraordinary thirty-year personal and professional partnership that survived the considerable strain of combining two families as well as long absences from home that required farming out the children to friends and relatives. John Szarkowski, who worked with the couple in the 1960s, said he came to realize that to a great extent "Lange's work was also [Taylor's] work." Clark Kerr, Taylor's friend, colleague, former student, and eventually university president, recalled that "Paul and Dorothea had complementary skills but contrasting personalities." Lange "was always moving, mostly talking, reacting in a flash," while Taylor "thought about everything, spoke seldom and then softly." Dorothea said that while Maynard Dixon "loved me and was very, very good to me," it was only after marrying Taylor that she realized "what it was to live with a person who shared their life with you." "Paul," she explained, "is my rock." After her death, Taylor believed that to have lived "thirty years with a woman like that is a gift that isn't given often to people. I had it. I still have it. What more could you ask from life?"

During the last half of the 1930s, Lange, often in collaboration with Taylor, produced a body of work that dramatically shaped America's image and understanding of the Depression. When Hollywood was preparing to film John Steinbeck's *Grapes of Wrath*, director John Ford turned to Dorothea's photographs to capture the proper look and visual feel of the movie. Her "Migrant Mother," the 1936 portrait of a Nipomo farm worker and her children, became one of the best-known photographs in the world and still symbolizes the Depression for millions of Americans. Lange and Taylor intended that *American Exodus*, a pictorial essay published in 1939, would be a popular summation of their Depression work. The book documented the great migration from the land caused by the economic crisis, but by the time it came out times were rapidly changing. Taylor explained that people were "turning their eyes to what we call the Defense Period," and the book sold poorly. By 1941 it was being remaindered for a dollar a copy.

In that same year, Dorothea became only the second photographer to receive a Guggenheim Fellowship. She planned a photographic study of the Amana, Hutterite, and Shaker communities but was forced to ask for a leave of absence to deal with her brother's arrest on fraud charges. By the time that matter was settled, the attack on Pearl Harbor had occurred, and Dorothea never did complete the fellowship project. She said that the nation was "in a different place;" going back to the project would have been returning to "something that was a relic."

"Shipyard years"

Dorothea called the early forties "the defense years, war years, shipyard years." The Bay Area experienced rapid mobilization, the bay itself becoming a virtual military reserve. Many East Bay installations like the Alameda Naval Air Station, the

Oakland Naval Supply Center, and the Oakland Army Base had been established in the 1930s, but after the attack on Pearl Harbor, they dramatically expanded. An African American Military Police camp was established near the foot of Ashby Avenue in Dorothea's hometown of Berkeley, and the university campus became the site of a naval officer training program. On a hill behind the campus where dairy cattle had grazed a few months earlier, the Radiation Laboratory, a giant facility helping to develop the atomic bomb, seemed to appear overnight.

The greatest impact on the region came from billions of dollars in defense contracts granted to Bay Area employers. While dozens of industries were affected, by far the largest beneficiaries were Bay Area shipyards. In 1939 the region's shipyard labor force numbered about 6,000. Five years later the figure was over 240,000, and the Bay Area had become the biggest shipbuilding center the world had ever seen. Over half the shipyard workers were employed in the East Bay, primarily at Moore Dry Dock Company in Oakland and the Kaiser yards in Richmond. Moore was an old-line operation whose work force climbed from 600 in 1939 to 30,000 in 1944. Kaiser was a brand new "instant shipyard," built for the wartime emergency. Although it hadn't existed in 1939, by 1944 Kaiser was the largest yard in the nation, employing nearly 100,000 workers.

The shipyard expansion occurred at a time when other industries were also booming, and ten to twelve million men and women were in the armed forces. The labor surplus of the Depression years rapidly turned into a drastic labor shortage. The Dust Bowl migrants immortalized by Dorothea's photographs were now welcomed into well-paying jobs at the shipyards. Employers urged retirees and students to join the work force, and one Bay Area shipyard even boasted that it had hired most of the members of the San Francisco Symphony Orchestra to work part-time.

When the local labor supply was inadequate, employers engaged in nationwide recruitment efforts, drawing new workers from all over the United States, particularly from the South and Midwest. Included were the founders of the Bay Area's first large black communities. Although there had been an African American presence going back to at least the Gold Rush, the region's black populations had remained small through the 1930s. All that changed in the forties. Between 1940 and 1944, Berkeley's African American population almost doubled, Oakland's grew by over two and a half times and Richmond's increased an astounding twentyfold. The economic boom also produced new waves of Mexican immigration, including workers imported through the *Bracero* program initiated by the U.S. government in 1942. Chinese Americans, who had been barred by discrimination from well-paid, unionized Bay Area industrial jobs for nearly a century, were now welcomed into the shipyard labor force.

One of the most dramatic changes in Bay Area life was the appearance of large numbers of women in what were formerly defined as male jobs. By 1945, at least a quarter of the blue collar, industrial workers at the Kaiser Richmond yards were female. One Kaiser woman worker remembered the yard as "a huge place, something I had never been in." There were "all these people from all walks of life, all coming and going and working. And there was a lot of noise. The whole atmosphere was overwhelming." But she also recalled "The salary was more than I'd ever made in my life." Although women and minorities received equal pay with white men within specific job categories, "glass ceilings" were very much in evidence. Of the tens of thousands of female shipyard workers in the Bay Area, only one was promoted to foreman. Still, as one black woman working in the defense industry put it, "Hitler was the one that got us out of the kitchen."

The pace of change was often traumatic for old residents of Bay Area communities. It was easy to blame the newcomers for all real and perceived problems. An Oakland newspaper argued that "when any city is suddenly overrun by a helter-skelter horde of newcomers… its older social barriers are inclined to be overturned and its cultural averages go backward." Some Oakland residents said they felt like tourists in their own hometown, and newspaper columns were filled with charges and countercharges between "natives" and "Okies." African Americans were particularly singled out for criticism, and tensions even appeared between old-timers and newcomers within the black community. One former Bay Area black resident remembered that "the old residents saw the new as crude, rough and boisterous." They lacked "manners and sense of decorum," and many of the old black residents wished the newcomers "would all go back where they had come from." But, of course, they stayed and laid the foundations of the large black communities that still exist in the region.

"The quiet horror of what she had been photographing"
Even as the "hordes" of newcomers were arriving, tens of thousands of other Bay Area residents were being required to leave their homes. This not only included

young men and women going off to war, but also all people of Japanese descent, who were forcibly interned at government "relocation centers," actually camps surrounded by barbed wire and guarded by armed men. President Roosevelt's Executive Order 9066, issued in February 1942, authorized military personnel to carry out the forcible relocation of people of Japanese descent, U.S. citizens and non-citizens alike, from the west coast of the United States. The order affected over 100,000 people, the majority of whom were American citizens and residents of California. Included were several thousand East Bay residents, mostly living in Oakland, Berkeley, and the agricultural communities of southern Alameda County.

Never charged with any crime or given their day in court, Japanese Americans were uprooted from their homes and communities with only a few weeks' notice. While most Bay Area residents, like most Americans, seemed to approve of the relocation, there were some criticisms of the action, particularly from a few Berkeley academics and community members. Several of Paul Taylor's current and former students were included in the relocation, and he opposed the policy from the outset, speaking out, signing petitions, and joining the Fair Play Committee, which tried to ameliorate some of the worst effects.

Dorothea also was passionately opposed, even though she accepted a position as a photographer for the War Relocation Administration, the government agency responsible for carrying out the relocation and operating the camps. According to Taylor, Lange believed that as a WRA photographer, she could document the injustice of the process. While most of her colleagues on the agency staff attempted to portray the removal in the best possible light, Dorothea's photographs presented a harsher view. She shot families before their forced removal and then followed the process through to the Manzanar camp. According to her assistant at the time, Lange was "overwhelmed by the quiet horror of what she had been photographing." Historian Roger Daniels believes that Lange succeeded in capturing the essence of the relocation process. "If we had to choose the work of just a single photographer to inform ourselves and posterity of what the wartime experience of Japanese Americans was like," he argues, "it would be that of Dorothea Lange." Apparently, the Army didn't agree. It impounded most of her WRA photographs, not releasing some of them until many years after the war. As Dorothea put it, "Although the Army wanted a record, it did not want a public record."

The WRA project marked the first full collaboration between Lange and Ansel Adams, the best known Bay Area photographer of his generation. During the thirties, Adams had been one of the organizers of f-64, a group of northern California photographers committed to photography as a pure and austere art form. Although the group consisted of some of her friends, including Imogen Cunningham, Dorothea was never a member, perhaps because she considered her pictures primarily social documents rather than works of art. Adams had been one of the first people to appreciate the importance of Lange's documentary work, calling her "an extraordinary phenomenon in photography." In 1934 he criticized her technique, but said he had "nothing but admiration for the more important things—perception and intention." Adams correctly predicted that "if any documents of this turbulent age are justified to endure, the photographs of Dorothea Lange shall most certainly." Although he had previously developed some of Lange's FSA negatives, the WRA project was the first time the two had worked as true collaborators.

Unlike Dorothea, Adams did not condemn the relocation, and generally his pictures showed the internees in pleasant and positive circumstances. His photographs of Manzanar emphasize the scenic grandeur of the site, while Lange's show the dusty, windswept environment of day-to-day camp life. Adams published a book of Manzanar photographs he hoped would create sympathy for the internees by portraying them as accepting their confinement with heroic cheerfulness. Dorothea believed the book was "shameful." According to her, Adams "gave the regular line, you know, but he wasn't vicious about it." "That's Ansel," she said, "he doesn't have much sense about such things." In the 1960s, Dorothea talked of the possibility of an exhibit of WRA photographs. After her death, her former assistant Richard Conrat and his wife Masie gathered 63 of the photographs into a book and exhibit entitled *Executive Order 9066*. Twenty-seven of the pictures were by Lange, by far the most of any photographer included. According to *New York Times* critic Hilton Kramer, "Miss Lange's work dominated the exhibit."

"Everything is propaganda for what you believe in"

In 1943 both Lange and Adams went to work for *Victory Magazine*, a publication of the federal Office of War Information, designed to "interpret the American spirit to war-torn Europe." The magazine was distributed in neutral countries and dropped into nations like Italy and Yugoslavia ahead of the allied troops. Dorothea's photographs accompanied articles on ethnic and immigrant communities in

California. Although the photographers received no credits in the magazine, her friend Beaumont Newhall recognized some of her pictures in a *Victory* issue he picked up while serving in Italy. After the war, federal authorities somehow lost all of Dorothea's OWI negatives, but her collection at the Oakland Museum includes examples of what she labeled as "rejects and duplicates" of at least some of the *Victory* photos. The pictures of *braceros* in this volume, for example, were probably taken as part of the OWI project.

Lange showed no discomfort at working for a government propaganda agency like the OWI. While some scholars have maintained that FSA photographers believed their work was purely objective, Dorothea at least accepted the subjective context of her images. She argued that "the line between fact and opinion in the hands of conscientious people is a fine line. Everything is propaganda for what you believe in, actually, isn't it? Yes it is." Ansel Adams maintained that what Lange believed in was "very party line... she had very strong sympathies." Paul Taylor adamantly denied Adams's implications of Communist sympathies, but Dorothea admitted that during the early thirties she might well have joined the party had it not been for Maynard Dixon's opposition. Clark Kerr, who called her "one of the most nonideological persons I have ever known," believed that even if she had joined, she would have never accepted party discipline.

Kerr is probably correct. Lange was constantly rebelling against Roy Stryker, her boss at FSA, and her government handlers at WRA and OWI. Her pictures display personal compassion rather than ideological conformity. She identified with workers and the poor, with people she believed to be underdogs and oppressed. Some scholars attribute these sympathies to her lifelong disability, but her collaboration with Taylor also profoundly affected her political sensibilities. Therese Heyman, Curator of Photography at the Oakland Museum, comes closest to the truth about Dorothea's politics when she describes Lange and Taylor as "earnest liberal believers." They "brought their art and creative talent to do a job they thought was possible, look for truth, explain it, and ask for solutions."

"It was a hometown once"

While Dorothea was working for the WRA and OWI, she was also photographing on her own, trying to capture images of the extraordinary social transformation going on around her. She walked the streets of downtown Oakland, a city which she said was "under war impact and changing fast now. It was a hometown once." The street life reflected the energy of the wartime boom. One recent arrival said, "My husband and I often walk the downtown streets after dinner just for the pure joy of the movement all about us." Dorothea stationed herself near the entrance of the cavernous Tenth Street Market to take dozens of shots of customers arriving and leaving. She was dissatisfied with the results: "Never did get anything very good," she said. It may be true that she never found the one, all-encompassing image that summed up the wartime social experience the way the "Migrant Mother" would sum up the Dust Bowl era; but as a group, the Tenth Street pictures convey a vivid sense of the demographic revolution enveloping Oakland during the war years.

The photographs particularly reflect the dramatic growth in African American population. A railroad and industrial city, Oakland had long had the largest black population of any Bay Area community. But as late as 1940, there were only about 8,000 black residents, less than three percent of total city population. By 1944 the number had grown to over 21,000.

Blacks were primarily attracted by the promise of good wages. One recent arrival from Arkansas left for the Bay Area when he heard "of the salary and money they were making in the shipyards." But African Americans also fled Southern states like Louisiana, Texas, and Arkansas to escape the rigid racism of the Jim Crow system. In Oakland and other Bay Area communities, blacks could vote and send their children to regular public schools, but they still faced substantial racial prejudice. Housing discrimination was chronic in the Bay Area, and blacks who were unable to find room in one of the hastily-built wartime public projects were forced to compete for housing in the few neighborhoods where minorities had traditionally been welcome. There was a substantial housing shortage for everyone, but it was far worse for African Americans because the available supply was so limited. In some neighborhoods, whole families lived in garages, and two or more workers shared a single bed (since the yards operated on three eight-hour shifts per day, one person could be sleeping in the bed while the others were working). West Oakland, adjacent to the Tenth Street Market, was one such neighborhood, and during the war it began its transformation from an ethnically diverse area to a largely black district. Even the government housing projects were internally segregated, with African Americans required to live in separate buildings within the larger complex.

In 1944 *Fortune* magazine hired Lange and Adams to shoot pictures for a major article on Richmond. Of all California cities, none was more dramatically affected by the war. It had been founded in the early twentieth century as an industrial town and by 1941 was home to several major employers, including Standard of California, Ford Motor Company, and Santa Fe Railroad. All of these facilities increased their labor forces substantially during the war, but the heart of Richmond's wartime economy was the Kaiser shipyards. Henry J. Kaiser owned an Oakland construction company and helped organize a consortium of western firms to bid on a number of important New Deal public works projects during the thirties. After 1939, Kaiser and his associates followed the trail of federal dollars into defense industries, including shipbuilding. It probably helped that they had no experience in the industry, for they were not wedded to traditional shipbuilding practices. Kaiser was willing to innovate, making use of prefabrication and pre-assembly processes, inventing assembly line techniques, and breaking down traditional shipyard crafts so that inexperienced, unskilled labor could produce ships faster than ever before in history. By 1944 Kaiser was the nation's biggest shipbuilder and Kaiser Richmond the nation's largest shipbuilding complex, with a labor force of nearly 100,000.

With the shipyards as the engine, Richmond experienced almost unbelievable growth during the war years. A working class town of about 23,000 overwhelmingly white inhabitants in 1940, just four years later it was a multi-ethnic city of 100,000 people, the black population growing from just 270 to nearly 6,000 in those years. 25,000 units of new housing were built, most by governmental agencies, but this wasn't enough to meet the demand, and war workers were living in trailer courts and chicken coops. New rail and ferry lines were constructed to transport workers to the yards. Schools operated on double or triple session, sometimes with as many as 60 students in a classroom. Hospitals, jails, playgrounds, and parks were overwhelmed. Traffic became hectic, and pristine marshes and tidelands were fouled by raw sewage flowing into the bay. Since the Kaiser yards operated 24 hours a day, with three eight-hour shifts, the city itself ran on a similar schedule, some businesses never closing at all. One observer said Richmond was "a city that looked like carnival night every hour for three years."

"Intricate aspects of workers' lives"
Dorothea was familiar with conditions in Richmond even before the *Fortune* assignment, since her brother and son worked at Kaiser. She and Adams were sometimes accompanied on their photographic shoots by her friends Homer and

Christina Page. Homer, who also worked at the Kaiser yards, recalled that Lange and Adams "were an impossible team, they were so unlike each other." Adams arrived with a station wagon-load of equipment and began the laborious task of setting up his platform, lights, and tripod. Dorothea, on the other hand, "with her usual Rolleiflex, an extra film bag, and a notebook," simply walked into the crowd and began shooting. Christina Page, who often drove Dorothea around Richmond (at about ten miles an hour so she wouldn't miss anything), remembered that Lange "had a peculiar facility for just melting away and for not seeming to be photographing at the same time she was sticking a camera in somebody's face." Lange believed she could cover herself with a "cloak of invisibility," a skill she learned as a young girl wandering around the dangerous streets of New York. "I knew how to keep an expression of face that could draw no attention, so no one would look at me." Adams, on the other hand, with a full beard and a ten-gallon hat, was hardly invisible. Homer Page argued that while Adams' pictures captured "the grandiose aspects of a great shipyard," Dorothea's caught "the intricate aspects of workers' lives."

Dorothea was fascinated by the life and energy of wartime Richmond and attempted to capture it in city street scenes. But she was also repelled by the way the great wartime labor migration was shattering families and communities. During the thirties, she and Taylor had been concerned with the breaking up of traditional rural farm and community life. Now World War II seemed to be finishing the job, drawing millions of Americans to unprepared, formless cities like Richmond. After Lange's death, Taylor published a new edition of *American Exodus*, including some of the Richmond photographs in a new chapter called "End of the Road: the City." Lange had proposed to study cooperative communities for her Guggenheim grant, and her perspective may have also been colored by her own sometimes troubled family life. In her Richmond photographs, she attempted to show the loneliness, rootlessness, and disorder of many of the shipyard workers' lives. Commenting on her images of workers leaving the Kaiser yards at a shift change, Dorothea wrote: "Notice how people are entirely unrelated to each other. This is the story of these times and the shipyards."

Lange knew that in the shipyards, the trade union movement provided little support and solace for the new arrivals. The Boilermakers Union was the chief shipyard labor organization, representing about 70 percent of the workers by the terms of a master agreement that affected most West Coast yards. It was a "closed shop" agreement, and workers were required to join the union before they could be employed. Unlike many progressive labor organizations in the Bay Area, the Boilermakers were an old-line, all-white craft union that had long prohibited African American membership. At Kaiser and other West Coast yards, black workers were forced to join all-black, Jim Crow "auxiliaries," which gave members the right to pay dues and little else. Not until early 1945 did the California Supreme Court declare the practice illegal in a case brought by workers at the Marinship yard in Sausalito, and by then shipyard employment was already beginning to decline. Even for white workers, the Boilermakers provided few services. In a commentary on her pictures of the union headquarters in Richmond, Dorothea wrote, "This was the introduction to the labor movement. Secondary unions—racial tensions. No formal business meetings. No democracy. Over 50,000 members pay 'tribute' in exchange for jobs.... A tragedy and a scandal of this war period in the Bay Area."

If unions often failed to meet shipyard workers' needs, elements of American popular culture did provide some sense of comfort and community. Many Southern and Midwestern white newcomers brought their love of country music to the region. (Bay Area natives often disparaged it as "hillbilly" music.) One worker from the Midwest remembered that "Dude Martin was big. It seemed like he played almost every night." Bay Area radio stations added country music programs, and established stars like Bob Wills appeared in both Oakland and Richmond. Jazz and blues clubs opened in Bay Area black communities, particularly in North Richmond and along Seventh Street in West Oakland. Both Southern white and black newcomers also brought a tradition of populist, evangelical religion, often practiced in hastily established storefront churches. There was even a gospel quartet, the Singing Shipbuilders, made up of four black Kaiser workers who met in a Richmond barber shop. They sang at African American services and had a weekly radio show on Berkeley's KRE. Typically, Lange photographed the newcomers' storefront churches and country music bars and clubs rather than the concerts and impressive houses of worship of established Bay Area natives.

"A dreadful fatigue... a physical tiredness"
In the spring of 1945, Dorothea was again working for the Office of War Information, photographing the founding meetings of the United Nations in San Francisco. She seemed to spend most of her time outside, shooting the delegates as

they wandered around the city, rather than at the formal sessions in the Opera House. She was on the streets the day Franklin Roosevelt died in April. During her U.N. assignment, Lange was increasingly troubled by severe stomach pains. When a doctor suggested that she take it easy, she replied, "Take it easy? How can a photographer take it easy?" In August, the same month the war finally ended, her body gave out and she entered the University of California Hospital for a gall bladder operation. The surgery was unsuccessful, and in September she hemorrhaged and was rushed back to the hospital. "It was a terrible time," Taylor recalled, "we thought we had lost her." Eventually, Dorothea was diagnosed with a duodenal ulcer and had a substantial portion of her stomach removed. The recovery was long and difficult, and Lange did not seriously practice photography again for eight years.

The end of the war in August of 1945 also brought an abrupt end to the shipyard boom. Kaiser Richmond and the other "instant" yards closed, and old-line firms like Moore went back to their pre-war levels of activity. Shipyard jobs disappeared almost overnight. One Kaiser worker remembered, "I don't think we had any warning at all.... You didn't get two weeks' notice or anything like that. You were just finished." Most of the former war workers found new jobs in the expanding post-war economy. But blacks had far greater difficulty than whites. Without wartime labor shortages and fair employment practices requirements, many employers were free to revert to traditional racist hiring policies. Recent African American arrivals from the South were often hampered by poor educational backgrounds and lack of skills. Most women war workers probably stayed in the labor market, but without access to unionized, blue-collar shipyard jobs, they were forced to accept much lower-paid "women's work."

The end of the war also marked the final victory of the automobile in Bay Area life. During the 1930s, federal funding had been available for major projects like the Bay Bridge and the first bore of what now is the Caldecott Tunnel. But during the thirties and early forties, few realized the full implications of those projects because of the effects of the Depression and wartime gasoline rationing. After the war, however, suburban housing tracts and shopping centers spread rapidly throughout the region. Supported by cheap FHA loans and promoted by new freeway construction, the suburban communities attracted an increasing share of the region's white middle class. Population and economic activity in the old central cities like Oakland and Richmond declined, and these communities became home to a high percentage of the East Bay's poor and minorities. The new suburban sprawl also transformed the landscape, paving over valuable farm land and destroying old agricultural communities that Taylor and Lange had studied during the thirties. When she was organizing her files in the 1960s, Dorothea commented that her pictures of wartime projects showed the "first tract housing (which was to spread more than we knew)."

Lange lived for another twenty years after World War II, often suffering illness, pain, and fatigue. Nevertheless, she took up photography again in 1953, producing a pictorial essay on an Alameda County public defender and a study of the Berryessa Valley before it was flooded by a federal dam. She also traveled to Utah and Ireland on assignment with *Life* magazine and took pictures while accompanying Taylor on government aid missions to several countries, including Vietnam. Finally, for the first time, Dorothea concentrated on photographs of her own family, taken at the Euclid Avenue home in Berkeley and her beloved weekend retreat at Steep Ravine on the Marin County coast.

Family concerns became increasingly important to her in these years. As if to make up for earlier absences, she presided over elaborate, almost ritualistic family gatherings and lavished attention on her grandchildren. Elizabeth Partridge, who was a virtual surrogate grandchild herself, appreciates the irony of "a woman who left her own children time and again, yet returned, gracious and full of magic to her grandchildren." Dorothea's son, Dan Dixon, observed that "with family and friends she instinctively maneuvered for control." "Her will," he recalled, "held our family together."

The illnesses and pain continued. In the early 1960s, Dorothea noted that "for the entire span of my life I have fought a dreadful fatigue… a physical tiredness." In 1964 she was diagnosed with inoperable cancer. She wrote to friends that "this time I shall not recover as I have been able to do many times before." She spent much of the last year of her life reviewing her collection of prints and negatives, choosing pictures for a personal retrospective exhibit. Although her photographs had often been included in prestigious group shows, including the "Family of Man" exhibition, the first extensive solo show of her works was scheduled for the Museum of Modern Art in New York in 1966. She completed the selection process for the show just a few days before her death in October, 1965. Her last words were, "Isn't it a miracle that it comes at the right time?"

Since her death, she has lived on most vividly in the memories of surviving family members and friends. Clark Kerr recalls that when he chatted with Paul Taylor over the years, "Dorothea's name would come up and Paul would sit there with tears streaming down his face." Dan Dixon still hears his mother saying, "Dan, what progress are you making? Why is it taking you so long? What are you doing with your life, today?" For the rest of us, Dorothea lives on through her photography, through pictures that Therese Heyman describes as having "an empathy so deep that it raises them to the level of art."

It is tempting to ask what Lange would make of the 1990s. How would her camera frame the homeless people on our streets, the new immigrants working in our cities and farms, the youthful graffiti on our walls? How would she react to politicians who seek out ethnic and immigrant scapegoats and blame the poor for their own poverty? Heyman has noted that Lange and Taylor (who died in 1984) "clung to the hope that what they were doing was part of the solution." But how would they, or for that matter, how would we define the solutions to the many problems of our time?

Perhaps the photographs in this book are a good place to start. Dorothea was photographing the beginnings of the era in which the majority of us have lived most of our lives, a fifty-year "Defense Era" in which military expenditures, policy, and politics affected every other aspect of California and national life. Now, as the Cold War winds down and the Defense Era ends, it is particularly appropriate to review Dorothea Lange's World War II images. In documenting the Second Gold Rush, Dorothea was photographing social processes that were to shape every part of our lives. In that sense, Dorothea was photographing a bit of all of us, of what we and our world were to become.

Sources

Most of the Dorothea Lange quotations in this essay are from notes that accompany her file of contact prints at the Oakland Museum or from her oral history, *The Making of a Documentary Photographer*, Suzanne Riess, Interviewer (Berkeley: Regional Oral History Office, Bancroft Library, University of California, 1968). Also valuable are Paul Taylor's oral history, *California Social Scientist*, Suzanne Riess, Interviewer (Berkeley: Regional Oral History Office, Bancroft Library, University of California, 1973), and two fine biographies, Milton Meltzer, *Dorothea Lange: A Photographic Life* (New York: Farrar, Straus, Giroux, 1978) and Karin Becker Ohrn, *Dorothea Lange and the*

Documentary Tradition (Baton Rouge: Louisiana State University, 1980). More recent works are Elizabeth Partridge (ed.), *Dorothea Lange: A Visual Life* (Washington: Smithsonian Institution, 1994), which contains excellent essays by Partridge, Clark Kerr, Roger Daniels and Dan Dixon, and *Dorothea Lange: American Photographs* (San Francisco: Chronicle Books, 1994) which includes equally good essays by John Szarkowski and Therese Heyman. Other sources on Lange are *Dorothea Lange* (New York: Museum of Modern Art, 1966), *Dorothea Lange* (New York: Aperture, 1981), James Curtis, *Mind's Eye, Mind's Truth: FSA Photography Reconsidered* (Philadelphia: Temple University, 1989), Dorothea Lange and Paul Schuster Taylor, *An American Exodus: A Record of Human Erosion in the Thirties* 2nd ed. (New Haven: Yale University, 1969), and Masie and Richard Conrat, *Executive Order 9066* (San Francisco: California Historical Society, 1972).

Major sources on California and the West during World War II are Roger Lotchin, *Fortress California* (New York: Oxford, 1992), and Gerald Nash, *World War II and the West* (Lincoln: University of Nebraska, 1990). By far the most valuable book on the East Bay during the war years is Marilynn S. Johnson, *The Second Gold Rush: Oakland and the East Bay in World War II* (Berkeley: University of California, 1993). Also valuable are some of the interviews in *On the Waterfront: An Oral History of Richmond, California,* Judith Dunning, Interviewer (Berkeley: Regional Oral History Office, Bancroft Library, University of California, 1991). Other sources on the Bay Area during World War II include Charles Wollenberg, *Marinship at War: Shipbuilding and Social Change in Wartime Sausalito* (Berkeley: Western Heritage, 1990), Katherine Archibald, *Wartime Shipyard: A Study in Disunity* (Berkeley: University of California, 1948), Joseph Fabry, *Swing Shift: Building the Liberty Ships* (San Francisco: Strawberry Hill, 1982), and Lawrence Crouchett, et al., *Visions Toward Tomorrow: The History of the East Bay Afro-American Community, 1852-1977* (Oakland: Northern California Center for Afro-American History and Life, 1989).

Photographing the Second Gold Rush

Executive Order 9066, signed February 19, 1942, authorized the removal of all people of Japanese descent from the West Coast.

Japanese American family, tagged and ready for relocation. Hayward, 1942.

Patriarch. Centerville (Fremont), 1942.

Oakland, 1942.

Lange wrote the caption: "Bienvenidos trabajadores Mexicanos." c. 1942.

Braceros, Mexican workers imported by the U.S. government to cope with the wartime labor shortage. c. 1942.

Pledge of Allegiance. c. 1942.

The wartime labor shortage produced new jobs for Chinese Americans, long victims of employment discrimination. 1943.

Shipyard worker. Richmond, 1944.

Lange called this young man "the Oklahoma Kid—shipyard worker." c. 1943.

The elderly, as well as the young, found shipyard jobs. 1944.

The African American population of Richmond grew twenty times during the war years. c. 1942.

Shipyard worker, Richmond. The labor shortage created opportunity for many. Lange commented: "Little boys went to work in the shipyards.... Their mothers and sisters, too." c. 1943.

According to Lange, the owner of this Berkeley shop "was on the way to the Richmond shipyards" to take advantage of the high wages. 1943.

Richmond shipyard workers on the San Francisco ferry c. 1943.

Workers at a bus stop near government housing. Richmond, c. 1942.

Parking lot at the Kaiser shipyards, Richmond, the world's largest
shipbuilding complex. c. 1943.

Beginning of a shift change at Kaiser shipyards in Richmond.

Shift change, Kaiser shipyards, Richmond

Lange commented: "Notice how these people are entirely unrelated to each other. This is the story of these times and the shipyard." c. 1942.

High cuisine, Kaiser shipyards. Richmond, c. 1943.

Lunch break, Kaiser shipyards. Richmond, 1943.

By the end of the war, women comprised about 25 percent of the
blue collar industrial work force at the Kaiser shipyards, Richmond.

The Boilermakers Union represented most West Coast shipyard workers. Lange called its undemocratic and racist policies "a tragedy and a scandal." c. 1943.

Paycheck line, Kaiser shipyards, Richmond. Workers earned $50 to $60 a week, good wages for the time. Women and minorities made equal pay with white men within specific job categories, but seldom if ever got promotions to more highly paid supervisory jobs. c. 1942.

Curbside conversation. Richmond, 1943.

All dressed up in downtown Richmond. c. 1943.

On MacDonald Avenue, streets and sidewalks were jammed day and night. Richmond, 1942.

Shoe store on MacDonald Avenue. Richmond, c. 1942.

MacDonald Avenue. Richmond, c. 1943.

MacDonald Avenue. Richmond, c. 1943.

Lange admired traditional street life. Telegraph Avenue. Oakland, 1943.

West Oakland scene, c. 1942.

Sreet scene. Oakland, 1942.

Near the Tenth Street Market, Oakland, c. 1942.

Tenth Street Market. Oakland, c. 1942.

Tenth Street Market, Oakland, 1944.

Tenth Street Market, Oakland.

Tenth Street Market. Oakland, c. 1942.

Tenth Street Market. Oakland, 1944.

Tenth Street Market. Oakland, c. 1942.

Tenth Street Market. Oakland, 1942.

Oakland street corner. 1942.

Newspaper vendor. Oakland, 1944.

Even the bees were mobilized. c. 1942.

Beef was severely rationed, horse meat wasn't.

Women, like this Berkeley mail carrier, moved into previously all-male occupations. 1944.

The influx of war workers overwhelmed the Bay Area housing supply. Families lived in garages, chicken coops, and trailer courts.

Home on leave at his El Cerrito trailer court. Lange reported that the soldier "has read Joyce, Farrell, Wolfe... wants to be a writer but has no education." Perhaps the G.I. Bill would eventually give him his chance. 1944.

Government housing projects, Richmond. Lange called the structures "Defense housing for the incoming hordes." c. 1944.

Shoeshine in the Richmond projects. c. 1943.

Churches sprung up to serve new residents. Richmond, c. 1943.

Entrance to an evangelical church. Richmond, c. 1943.

Street scene. Richmond, c. 1942.

Dude Martin in Richmond. New residents from the South and the Midwest brought "hillbilly music" to the Bay Area. c. 1942.

An all-night movie house, a refuge for lonely shipyard workers. Richmond, c. 1942.

A Richmond saloon. c. 1942.

Wartime social mobility and change put a heavy strain on families, including perhaps this couple. Richmond, c. 1943

New economic opportunities and wartime cultural changes transformed this young couple's world. MacDonald Avenue, Richmond, 1942.

Richmond schoolchildren responding to the question: "How many of you were *not* born in California?" These children would, in the years to come, build a new California. c. 1942.